KEEP YOUR LEGS CROSSED

AND OTHER ADVICE MY GRANDMOTHER GAVE ME

BY STEPH GOLD

COPYRIGHT

DISCLAIMER

Cover Design: John Matthews

Interior Design: Heidi Miller

Editing: Ginger Moran, Terri Mullins

Author's photo courtesy of Bonnie Nichoalds.

DEDICATION

I dedicate this book to Grandma Gold, who taught me so much during the time we spent together. Thank you for continuing to speak loudly from heaven; I have no problem hearing your advice and receiving signs that you continue to follow me on my journey. I also dedicate this book to those who have gone before me-grandparents, uncles, aunts, cousins, and most recently my father. I love and miss you all dearly.

TABLE OF CONTENTS

INTRODUCTION

My grandmother and I had a special connection that began even before I met my parents. I was adopted from an agency in Saint Louis. My parents had been on the adoption list for four years before I was born. Since her son was on the list for adopting a baby, my grandmother attended an open house to tour the facilities. After the tour was complete, one of the head ladies asked her if she would like to see the nursery. She accepted the invitation, and was led into a room where all the new babies laid in their cribs. Gram walked over to a crib, peered inside, and saw me. The woman offered to let her hold the baby, and Gram gladly accepted. She explained to me how incredibly emotional the experience was for her, because it was in that moment that she knew in her heart I would be her grandchild. Sure enough, my parents received the call days after Gram held me, and I was placed with my mother and father.

The connection between my grandmother and myself was always strong. She understood me in a way that is indescribable. I often felt she knew me better than I knew and understood myself. I ran to her for everything. As a child, when I would argue with my parents, she was my first call. I would threaten to "run away," and Gram would offer to come pick me up. Looking back, I realize how ridiculous I was acting, but Gram never made me feel that way. She would listen for as long as I needed, and then give me her honest opinion. She would do so in the softest, most loving tone and no matter what her advice was, I respectfully accepted it.

She had a way of saying what I needed to hear, and not what I wanted to hear. We remained close throughout grade school, into high school, through college and beyond. She was so supportive, attending plays at school, recitals, and remained actively involved in my life. After college, I stayed in Texas for a year. After coming to the realization that I was hiding out from my father's illness and actually had no purpose in Texas, I moved back to Saint Louis. I spent an entire summer living off savings and partying every night. I watched all ten seasons of "Friends" that summer. Finally, my savings ran out, and I was in desperate need of a job to pay bills and survive. I spent a day on Craigslist and went on the first interview I was offered. The position was for pre-school teaching. I had gone to school for Communications. My passion and goals had been to write a book, do motivational speaking, and life coaching for as long as I can remember. The age group I have adored for years was teenage age girls. I had absolutely zero desire or certification to work with preschool children. Regardless, my communication skills helped me nail the interview, and I was given the position.

The preschool was brand new, and the owner hired far too many staff members. As a result of slower enrollment than expected, I was let go. I made next to nothing in the short time I worked for the school. I recall leaving the school that day absolutely heartbroken. I felt like such a failure, dreaded facing my parents and was so disappointed in myself. I left school and drove straight to Grandma's. Hysterically crying, ashamed, and disappointed.

She sat me down and listened as I babbled. I tumbled out how I felt like a failure. She took one look at me, smiled and said, "Stephy, you never wanted to be a pre-school teacher. This job was never something you worked for or wanted." I stopped crying and thought about what she was saying. She was entirely correct. I was not upset that I was fired from a job I never wanted; I was scared because now it meant I would have to take the gamble and risk of going after my dreams! Gram and I spent the rest of the afternoon hanging out and laughing. I cherish the memory of that day, and how quickly she switched the disappointed chaotic emotion that had filled my head to the comfort and ease of knowing exactly where I was headed.

I truly did not appreciate the life lessons my grandmother consistently modeled until she was making her way to Heaven. Sitting by her bedside and journaling, I recall going over her many stories in my head, and trying to make sense of them. As I wrote them down and considered all the joy she had given all of her loved ones, I began to see similarities; common threads that would help map out lessons to live by. You see, Gram was my go-to in tough times, times of contemplation, and times of growth. I would always rely on her advice to help me through, show me direction, and guide me to answers on how to deal with various events throughout my life. The thought of losing someone so significant was absolutely unbearable, but I was determined to keep her spirit alive by passing on her advice, guidance, life wisdom and knowledge.

The similarities I found turned into steps, rules almost, on how to live; an outline so to say, to help guide me with her infinite wisdom when I was without her voice. I do not have it all figured out, each day is a constant challenge, but having these steps and tools provides me comfort that I will have her guidance with me always.

As the days passed when Gram was in hospice, I listened and I heard many friends and family fear as I did that her stories and humor would be lost once she left us. To everyone she encountered, she was this beacon of light and hope, a symbol of joy and happiness each of us looked forward to seeing. All of these people seemed terrified to lose everything she was to them in their lives. I heard many individuals say, "She lived such a happy life," and, "What will we do without her jokes and laughter?" From what everyone was saying, it seemed as though all of these joyous gifts would die with Gram. I remember becoming passionate about the fact that it was our job, the job of those who knew her and were touched by her soul, to keep her alive. Those who knew her needed to carry on her spirit and live life the way she did, to help inspire those they encounter that did not have the opportunity to meet her. I also realized that Gram did not live a "happy life" because life always worked out for her and hard situations did not arise. It was indeed the opposite. She lived a happy life because of the way she viewed situations. Things happened that were entirely out of her control. Awful situations occurred in her life, illness and loss, but she never spent time focused on the negative. Difficult situations happened and instead of attempting to control them, she embraced them. No matter what was going on she chose to see the positive, flick off the negative, and move on.

During some of the many conversations we shared in her living room on a Sunday afternoon, Gram made a comment to me a few times that really stuck. She said, "People today do not seem as happy as they used to." She did not know why nor did she ever try to guess. She was not sure what the cause was, however, she was confident that people in the past were happier. I became determined to get to the bottom of why. What has changed so drastically in the last fifty or so years that would cause people to become less joyful? One of the conclusions I have come up with has led me to writing this book. With the rise of technology and increase in fast food restaurants, we have become a society that expects results immediately. We are less patient, less thoughtful. I believe that all of this running around and desire for instant gratification has caused us a lot of anxiety. I watch people lose their cool over the smallest of setbacks. When situations occur that are a deviation of the schedule we demand, often we spiral into a tornado of anxiety. Have you ever watched as someone's screen goes blank on his or her phone and the device will not turn on? You can watch as a wave of anxiety comes over, he or she and the individual must immediately stop all else in life to solve this problem. Working with children, I have watched as countless kids cry over the fact that they are not allowed to take their phone or iPad to bed with them. We laugh, but this is a real issue. We are raising a generation that has a constant need to be connected and dialed in even while they are sleeping, or worse yet, not sleep at all because they will stay up all night playing. I know I have been guilty of sleeping near my phone, waking up to my phone, even checking it before I get out of bed. With all this "connection" we now have to the entire world, constantly, are we missing out on the people and experiences right in front of us? Are we losing sight of the conversations, people, and experiences that truly matter? Are we angering too easily, and spending too much time becoming frustrated at frivolous details that do not actually matter?

My Grandmother was the happiest individual I have encountered. Having mentioned that it was not the details or events in her life that brought her such immense joy but instead, her happiness was a result of her perspective. I am determined to help others achieve optimal joy and positivity in their lives through modeling her approach. While on this mission of delivering Gram's perspective and lessons to others, I have taken special notice of situations where I feel greater joy or positivity can be inserted. A few months ago, I attended my younger cousin's graduation from college. Followed by the family gathering for a beautiful dinner. After dinner, the graduate's sister, brother-in-law, boyfriend, and myself went back to her apartment. Thirty minutes or so went by before I realized the girls were not talking; all three of us were on our phones and not interacting with one another. I had a moment of enlightenment and realized, I rarely see these two girls, and I was embarrassed that we were not interacting during the limited time we would have together. I asked if my cousin had a deck of playing cards or any games, and she did not. I then recalled a hilarious app called "Heads Up." I asked if either of the girls had the game on their phone. Sure enough my cousin did, and the three of us began to play. The game is incredibly interactive and involves being timed. There is a portion of the game that requires individuals to act out a concept or idea while the other person guesses. We had so much fun with this game and were becoming so competitive and enjoying ourselves tremendously. After some time, the guys asked if we were ready to leave. When we looked at the clock, we realized three hours had disappeared without any of us having a slight idea we had been playing longer than thirty minutes. I look back and am so grateful for that time the three of us spent together laughing. I imagine what our time together may have looked like had we not played that game. All of our heads down, looking and reading information we all most certainly could have seen later or never seen at all, and that most likely would not have mattered what so ever in our lives. I am so grateful we now share this fond memory of our time together at her graduation that I know we will continue to speak of when we see one another. The memory of our fun time will encourage us to interact earlier when we are around one another, than it would have had we not had this experience.

I believe a number of these distractions involving technology and our desire to receive information instantly contributes to a decline in our happiness overall and I am determined to insert more joy and laughter into our lives. I believe awareness is key here. By being aware of the fact that no one was interacting in her apartment, I was inspired to think of ideas on how to change that. None of us were enjoying ourselves while we were focused on the nonsense that we were reading on our phones; to be honest, we were all about to fall asleep. Once we began playing the games and interacting with one another, we each found joy and a burst of energy and excitement. Technology will not go away and it is an incredible tool, it did of course provide the game we were playing. I believe the importance is understanding how and when to use technology and having the awareness to recognize when and how it is appropriate for optimal joy. Being aware of the fact that you are sitting in a room having a conversation with your 94-year-old grandmother, who will one day be gone, and understanding in that moment that the texts, calls, insta posts, snapchats, tweets, Facebook posts, and all else coming in can wait, is key. I am so glad that I had a Grandmother who would yell, "Put that phone away." I think the anxiety comes from the feeling that we will miss an invitation or gossip. What is going on that I am not aware of? Who may be trying to reach me? Ultimately, through studying the life of my Grandmother I appreciate that humans survived a long time in a positive way without carrying around computers in their pockets, and I believe the more we open our eyes to what is right in front of us, the more joyful our lives will be.

CHAPTER 1:
FIND THE LAUGH

"Keep your legs crossed and your zipper up!"

Gram's signature line was, "Keep your legs crossed and your zipper up." She used it constantly, leaving stores, doctor's offices, to the mailman, family members, grandchildren's boyfriends or girlfriends-anyone leaving her home. She said it constantly, and to anyone and everyone she encountered throughout her day. More often than not, it was used as a departure line. More common phrases when leaving are often: "Goodbye," "See you later," "Have a nice day," "Bye, thank you," but who remembers that? I do not recall the thousands of people who have bid me farewell in those ways, but I can almost guarantee not a soul has forgotten my grandmother leaving and yelling out "Keep your legs crossed and your zipper up," and sometimes if you were really lucky, even "...and keep your nose clean." I can only assume many grandmothers end their conversations with "I love you," but Gram knew there was never any question about the love between herself and whom she was talking to, so she chose a different departure phrase.

She enjoyed saying it, because every time she said it, the words made her chuckle. Part of the joy was seeing the startled expression on the faces of people receiving the message. Usually it was shock, followed by laughter. Can you imagine a 90-year old woman kindly—yet almost sternly—saying these words to you?

I listened for years as Gram told me stories—stories of all kinds. I always left the room after one of her stories laughing out loud. When I think about some of the memories she shared and consider for a moment how it would feel to personally go through that experience, I realize finding the humor in that situation took skill. It may have been a skill that came naturally for her, but not for me. I think, especially in this busy time we live in, we rank instant gratification as a necessity. The gift of finding humor in a minor annoying setback is a practice and daily struggle I plan to master as completely and effortlessly as she did. Gram encountered many mishaps while raising four boys, but she handled them with laughter.

The Gold boys put undesired food, insects, outdoor creatures and just about anything else in their pockets. With four adventurous little ones running around in all directions, you can imagine the things she would discover while doing the laundry. Many times it was mashed potatoes or whatever vegetable had been served that evening for dinner, but this time was much more exciting. She threw in the laundry and neglected to check pockets. When she came back later, and opened the lid to the machine, she saw brown and pink lines all over the inside. What was it? As she peered in to take a closer look, she realized the lines were worms. I mean it makes perfect sense, right? Don't you, too, put worms in your pockets? One of her boys had been fishing, and had placed the worms he used to lure the fish, in his pockets. Think for a minute, before I describe her reaction, just how you would feel opening the lid of the washing machine and finding this. You have a million tasks you are juggling throughout the day, the boys are coming home soon, you have dinner yet to make, and you have just opened your washing machine and found all your clothes covered in disgusting worms.

Finding worms in the washing machine is the definition of a bad day. You know in that moment you would be less than thrilled. It would be extremely easy to be irritated for the rest of the night, yell at the kids when they walked in the door, call some friends and bitch about how awful and annoying it was to pull clothes out covered in worms, and when your husband walks in the door from a long day, complain to him. Worms in the wash would be a serious annoying setback, and worthy of complaining about. What is funny though, is that is not the story I heard. The story I heard was not that of the worst day or even a slight annoyance. When Gram would tell that story she would say, "And you know what I thought when I opened that lid?" with a warm belly chuckle, "All I could think about were those poor worms." She would finish by saying, with a laugh, "Those poor things never saw that coming." She would move her neck in a circular motion with her eyes wide and say, "I bet they were thinking, where the hell are we..." as they spun around and around. She laughed and felt sorry for those poor worms. Her humorous interpretation of the event, became one that would be told for generations. She turned what could easily have been a bad day into an adorable and hilarious story of what life was like raising four boys.

Stories like that were how I grew up learning about what life was like when my dad was growing up, in a house with all boys. I think about how easy it would be to be negative about that situation. I think about the parts of that story I never heard about, cleaning the clothes out, washing the machine after getting out the worms, all the extra time it took to clean the machine and all the clothing. I have a strong feeling though, that as she performed the task of cleaning she continued to think of the worms and laugh the entire time. How beautiful it is, to laugh through the entire process instead of angrily going through the motions and continuing to stress and become worked up. If she had not found a way to laugh about that situation, I wonder if it would have been a story I would have ever heard. Do we want to look back and remember moments of anger and frustration, and then tell our grandchildren those stories when we age? Or do we tell them the stories of the times we laughed and found joy? I wonder, when considering that story and the extreme difference in viewing those series of events, how many times have we all let a funny story slip away by masking it with anger, and creating a story we would never want to remember or tell again.

Situations arose in her life, the way they do, that were not pleasant. At times, things were hard. Shit happened to Gram, just as it does to all of us. She knew how to find the laugh and turn crap into humor. I can even recall a time when my brother had found Grandpa's tool kit one night when we were at her house for a sleepover. Gram was on the phone chatting with a friend, and I was coloring on the floor. Ryan, my brother, had to have been two or three. He grabbed a pair of pruners that were in the box, pulled up some wires from under the carpet on the staircase, and cut them. Gram's phone call immediately disconnected. She came in to check on us, and found Ryan with wires and pruners in hand. She gasped and he responded, "Gam ma, I fix it." Gram burst out laughing, took the tool from Ryan and said with a chuckle, "Well, I guess I was finished with that phone call." With that, she took us upstairs and we laid in bed reading books and telling stories.

I rarely saw her angry or frustrated. I think that is why I can recall so many of these stories. I have blocked out many of the times people were genuinely angry with me, or the times a situation ended in a scary, upsetting way. We block those memories out because they are not enjoyable. They do not bring us happiness or comfort. I would imagine it would be pretty frustrating to have had your phone line cut,

I am sure many can relate to missing their cell phone, the screen going black, it neglecting to turn on, the panic that comes over us when that occurs. But why? Are we actually in an unsolvable, unsafe situation when technology cuts us off briefly from the outside world and the things that are not currently right in front of us? What if we all viewed those instances as an opportunity? Ryan, Gram, and I did not spend the rest of the evening running to the neighbors and making calls to family, friends, and the telephone company. Gram took it as an excuse to stop chatting with a friend and to instead spend time with my brother and me.

I can recall a time Gram was over at the house watching me. Gram had brought her little sidekick Shih Tzu, Mercedes, with her to the house. She was facilitating a play date with one of my close friends, Christine. My friend and I, both deprived of family dogs at the time, were elated to have a little furry friend to play with. After hours of messing with this little pup, she became tired of us. She was use to Gram's temperament, and I am sure annoyed to be entertaining two little girls. Mercedes finally snapped. Unfortunately, she chose Christine. Christine was this adorable, brown curly haired, sweet little girl who would never hurt a fly. She was the prettiest little girl, probably only seven or eight, with freckles dusted across her nose. Thankfully, it was just a snip on the nose, no blood, or scratch for that matter, just a startled little girl who started to cry. Gram took one look at this sweet girl, and opened her arms wide for Christine to accept a warm embrace. Gram hugged her gently for a brief moment, and then pulled back, "Let me see you, sweetie." As Gram looked close, her voice changed from soft and caring to abrupt and cheerful. She leaned her face in to examine the targeted area and as she spoke Christine stopped crying and we both leaned in to listen intently. "Mercedes bit off one of your freckles." She peered in even closer, "Yes, she absolutely did. One of your freckles is missing." We both burst out laughing. How quickly Christine's tears turned to laughter! What a gift Gram had.

I think about this situation now, how many different reactions there could have been. I have worked with numerous families over the last eighteen years, and I have studied and watched parent/child interaction. I have to say that there are many more common reactions than that which my grandmother displayed. For instance, the overreaction, the one that almost terrifies the child even more, and leads him or her to believe he or she is more hurt than actuality. There is also, of course, the lack of reaction, leaving the child feeling uncared for, unheard and most often leading him or her to cause a larger display than necessary in hopes of gaining some sort of response or attention. I would say those are the most common.

Christine and I, still friends, recall this instance and speak of it when Gram is mentioned. This encounter happened at least twenty years ago, and we still look at it as a fond memory. A fond memory! I feel funny even typing those words, but it is true. I think about how common this situation is, it was not a big enough deal to really make an impact. There was no blood drawn, scrape, scratch, nothing.

The event was insignificant. Therefore, had Gram reacted in a common way, I highly doubt it would have remained a topic of conversation or something either of us would even recall. What made it memorable was my grandma's humorous spin. It became a fond memory because we laughed so hard. We continue to talk about it because it continues to make us smile and laugh.

Gram was the absolute best at taking a serious or scary situation and finding the humor. In her early 80's Gram was experiencing shortness of breath. She was told by her doctor that she was in need of heart surgery to replace a valve. Hearing news of major surgery is enough to worry a person of any age however Gram saw this situation as an opportunity to laugh. She asked the doctor what type of valve he would put into her heart, knowing it was a pig's valve. When he responded "Pig's valve" her reply was, "Oh no honey that won't work, I'm Kosher." After the two shared a laugh, the doctor explained the risks involved in the procedure and then noticed on her chart that she was at an age they would not usually perform that type of procedure. She was confident and never felt her age until her last year on earth. She had the procedure, and lived for more than ten years after it.

Later, in her early 90s, she had a doctor's appointment. I can only assume this appointment was less than routine, because both of her living sons were present. To be honest, I never heard anything about the details of the appointment. I could not tell you what was discussed between her and the doctor, or why it was important for her sons to be present. The next time I visited with Gram, I recalled dad telling me he had accompanied her and Uncle Terry to an appointment. I asked my grandmother how her doctor's appointment went. "Well," she said with a huge grin on her face. "The doctor walked into the room and asked me how I was doing in front of Terry and Rick.." (her sons) "And I said, 'Well, my eyelids have dropped, my chin has dropped, my boobs have dropped, and my bladder has fallen, what you see is what you get." After the doctor "came to" as she so delicately put it, he looked at Rick and Terry and they both smiled and shrugged. She said her sons were barely fazed by her response, but her shocked young doctor hardly knew how to reply. He then turned to her and said, "Well, Mrs. Gold, I think I may be able to help you with at least one...maybe two of those things." She joked and told me that she thought he did not want to see her again so badly that if anything bothered her she could call in and he would immediately write her a script. "I think I could call in for cocaine and I would get it," she joked. "Just so he does not have to see me." Then she reminded me, "I always say, get a young doctor and an old lawyer." Her thought was that you need a doctor who knows all the latest teachings and you need a lawyer that knows all the ins and outs. She was amazing in turning a simple question into a hilarious story. Being in one's 90s, doctor visits are not exactly an activity one would look forward to. I know her eyes began to fail her, and watching television and reading the paper presented a challenge in her later years, but when we spoke her focus was never on those failings.

Laughter always seemed to guide her. Always smiling, telling funny stories, or laughing, she never appeared to have a care or fear in the world. One of my all time favorite moments witnessing her famous departure phrase was when she was exiting the hospital. After an extended stay in the hospital and with her health not improving, the family decided to have her move to a hospice location where she would be more comfortable. I was in the room with her when the paramedics came to transfer her to the nursing home. Her eyes were closed and she appeared to be sleeping peacefully when they arrived. A nice young male paramedic said sweetly in her ear, "Ma'am, can you cross your arms for us? We are going to move you to this stretcher." Sure enough, she crossed her arms, they moved her, and started for the door. As they entered the hallway they were greeted by doctors and nurses running in and out of patient's rooms, as well as, family members of various patients in the hall. It was a busy area. With Gram's eyes still closed, she yelled out, to anyone and everyone who could hear, "Now keep your legs crossed and your zipper up…all of you!"

The initial reaction was silence, then laughter filled the halls. What a way to leave the hospital and to thank all of the staff for their help and service: laughter. I imagine for her that took effort, given she had not said much of anything for some time, and had appeared to be resting. How wonderful to leave the hospital and make those people in the hallway laugh and in return to receive the gift of laughter and support as she continued her journey to hospice. "Keep your legs crossed and your zipper up" was her way of saying, "Bye, thank you." She always said "goodbye" with this signature saying. It made everyone laugh, no matter how many times they had been told it by her. Those that knew and loved her always felt her love and she would tell us she loved us, but mostly she was able to use humor to communicate the same emotion.

After she left the hospital that day, when she was being moved to hospice, the paramedics took her to a beautiful nursing home where she would lie comfortably during her final days. Once she arrived at the hospice location, my aunts, my mother and I joined her. The nurse came in with the new patient paperwork. Gram lay in her bed peacefully. The room was decorated in gorgeous gold and deep red tones; it was warm and inviting. We had a lamp on by the bed, and light gently poured in from the hall. With one of my aunts on each side, and mom and I at the foot of her bed, she was surrounded by love. I massaged her feet over the blanket, in hopes of keeping her comfortable. As the lady read down the list of questions and features of the center, Gram quietly listened, eyes mostly closed.

When it came to the food and beverage portion of the paperwork, she perked up for a second. "I like a glass of wine at five and when is happy hour?" This night would mark the beginning of the final days of her life, and she would no longer be partaking in drinking alcohol. However, to hear her say phrases like this brought us all comfort, and I trust it brought her comfort, as well.

My grandmother truly had a gift. She was able to insert humor and create laughter out of all types of situations. I am by no means suggesting what she accomplished was easy. For me, it is much easier to get upset, write myself a sob story or wallow in my misery. Sometimes I think it is appropriate to give yourself time to do those things. However, the more memorable reaction, enjoyable, and laughter-provoking interpretation of life, and all its crazy events that take place, is what creates memories worth telling again. Most of these stories are insignificant without the added humor. When I was writing Gram's eulogy, I looked over these stories and realized it was not the facts that made any of these fond memories or even interesting tales. Honestly, most I cannot imagine I would even recall or would be worthy of mentioning if it was not for the way she added humor so deliberately and gracefully into the lives of others. She was like a laugh messenger, inserting joy into all the lives she came in contact with. Her gift required awareness of her surrounding, attention to the lives passing her on her journey, and above all else, an ability to focus on joy and humor rather than her own pain, fear, or suffering.

It is easy to become wrapped up in the details of life. Small annoyances that appear to get in the way of our plans can quickly become an excuse for anxiety to kick in. I have found that stepping back in that moment, although often difficult, has allowed me to see the humor and laughter life is offering in that moment. I continue to find laughter more enjoyable than anxiety, time and time again. Annoyances that interfere with my schedule or daily timeline can easily result in my becoming worked up. I find if I become worked up, my annoyance will quickly turn into a topic of conversation and a story I find myself telling girl-friends or my mother. Instead of allowing a negative place or detail to become my focus, Gram's approach is what I strive for. She taught me it is easy to get caught up in the busy details of life. It is easy to take life too seriously. For me, the ability to find humor in frustrating situations is a tool that requires effort and polishing in my life. I practice it frequently because it does not come easily for me. It is much easier for me to get frustrated and end up spending time talking to friends about the things that are frustrating me and consuming my thoughts. Often, I have walked away from a conversation or hung up the phone and thought, was that enjoyable for them? How did they perceive that conversation? Everyone knows a person that constantly complains; we all have at least one of those individuals in our lives. I work hard not to be that person. I find it so much more enjoyable to make the situation funny and tell the story that contains a laugh. That is the story people will want to hear again and will remember. What a better impression to leave with them. Gram displayed effortlessly that inserting laughter could be as simple as a signature departure phrase, and as complex as turning an annoying, or scary situation into a humorous event.

CHAPTER 2:

MAKE TIME FOR PLAY

"We had a bridge club, we called the Bitch Club."

The joyful life my grandmother led is a constant reminder to make time for play. She incorporated a wildly playful imagination into her parenting style and later her grandparenting style. She prided herself on having playful décor not for anyone else's approval but her own. She had a unique way of decorating her home that allowed her to be happy in her space. Gram had a way of making everyday whether it was an ordinary day or holiday playful and enjoyable throughout her entire life.

Gram surrounded herself with individuals who appreciated her playful take on life. She had a group of friends that would get together to play Bridge. They called themselves the "Bitch Club" because they would sit around and bitch, the way girlfriends do. She never did attempt to alter her word choice to make it "appropriate" for those around her. She was who she was, and if you did not like it she would offer you her middle finger.

Raising four boys presented an opportunity for that playful side of hers to shine in many ways. Gram had another name for herself, "Mary Hoopenfoodle." This name had come about after tirelessly hearing four boys repeat the title "mom," to gain her attention. She described that hearing "mom" over and over again would become exhausting. In a store one day, she had heard it repeated so many times that finally she turned to the boys and in a calm and serious manner said, "I am not your mother, I am just a woman that looks a lot like your mother, my name is Mary Hoopenfoodle." She described the priceless faces of the boys, the furrowed brows, wide eyes, and clear fear and confusion across their young faces. Instead of yelling, becoming angry, or any other common response, she chose to have a little fun with her response. This story, along with the name "Mary Hoopenfoodle," stuck with her throughout her life. Her grandchildren would later call her "Mrs. Hoopenfoodle" from time to time, or address her mail that way.

When my dad and his brothers were young, Gram had an extra stocking hanging from the mantel at Christmas time. She said the stocking was for "nobody." Having four boys in the house, she explained to me, that mishaps and accidents were always happening or going wrong. There was constant excitement, but when she would go to ask who had done the mishap, none of the boys would fess up. Therefore, it was always "nobody's" fault. Since "nobody" was playing such a crucial role in the family's daily lives, Gram decided to hang a stocking for this "nobody" who was always mentioned.

I just love this so much. Think about how easy it is to become worked up. I recall all of the children I have worked with over the years and how incredibly annoyed or angry I have become if the children are not confessing to something that has been broken, spilled, etc. Displaying the easier reaction, most of the time, resulted in a more worked up version of myself, maybe even another sob story I wrote myself about how the children misbehaved and none of them would admit to who did what. Gram had it right. Turn the event into something playful. If everyone is saying "nobody" did it, then let us honor "nobody." She had such a clever way of letting the boys know she was onto them. I think of how it has felt to have the easier over reaction—awful, frustrating, angry. Then I think of how it would feel to follow Gram's approach, humorous, enjoyable, and overall happy.

Gram was witty and playful when parenting but also with her home décor. My dad worked for a travel company for 39 years. When he first started working as a Travel Director, he was in his mid-20s. As a result of traveling three out of every four weeks a month, his home base remained his parents' house, during his first years in the business. He was traveling all over the world and would find interesting or unique artwork and buy one for himself and one for his mom. My grandma kept many of these little treasures dad brought home. She stored carved whalebone he brought her in her china cabinet until the day she died.

She loved oriental influenced artwork, and had many pieces. Her home was filled with animal artwork and trinkets. Grandma had quite a collection of elephants. She also loved small dogs and had many small dog figurines. Gram enjoyed funny sayings and had many hanging in various places in her home. She loved Buddha's and had a very special one, which was displayed on the floor and was delightfully named "Happy Buddha." The Buddha had the best expression on its face of sheer laughter. She absolutely loved it and this particular statue made her extremely happy.

As a child I can recall a large stuffed dog Gram kept outside on the porch. She called the dog Casey. From the street, Casey looked like a real dog. Some were scared of Casey, some impressed with the fact that he would remain sitting outside Gram's door for hours. I think, initially, she put the dog out there to decorate on a nice day. Then, because of how much attention Casey received, she kept him out there. Casey even had a spread in the paper! The paper read, "Today there was no trouble at the Gold home. The police didn't check to see if the dog was off the leash. The mail carrier didn't refuse to deliver the Gold family bills. No trash collectors, meter readers, or delivery drivers cautiously approached the section of sidewalk the mutt staked out." Gram was absolutely tickled by people's reactions, and so was my grandfather. My family has kept many copies of this article. The image is of my Grandpa, Grandma, their living Shih Tzu, and stuffed Casey in the paper with the title "The Perfect Polyester Pet and Watchdog." The article serves as hilarious reminder of Gram's unique decorating skill, and desire to have fun with life.

Every inch of her home was decorated with unique trinkets. Her personality was so rich in character that it was easy to pick out something that reminded you of her. It was always something that would make her laugh, usually brightly colored, and almost always completely inappropriate. People always enjoyed Gram's décor and her clearly playful attitude toward decorating her space. Decorating, however, was not the only time her playful side was displayed.

Taking ordinary events and adding play was something Gram did effortlessly, so you can only imagine how holidays were celebrated. Halloween was a favorite of my grandmother's. She lived in a house with a spiral staircase, so the outside had an amazing looking tower. As a child, I referred to her home as the "castle house." It was gorgeous during the day, but at night it may have been a little scary to a child, especially on Halloween. The ivy growing up the sides and large bushes in the front would cast scary shadows on the side of the house at night. As children trick or treating would near her home to ring the doorbell, Gram would jump out of the large bushes in front of the porch stairs, dressed as a witch, and yell "boo." The children would scream and run away. She did not do this just one time; this was her annual Halloween routine.

So playful and young at heart, my grandmother also especially enjoyed Christmas time very much. She put up a large tree every year. Tons of small elves would cover the mantel, and she would tuck them into different areas of her home, in the blinds, on a chair, next to the sugar bowl. She was so creative when it came to her décor, and always had all her grandchildren in mind. Once her boys had children and the family's Christmas celebration grew, my grandmother really enjoyed celebrating all together, as a family. We would gather at her place on Christmas Eve. Gram would remind us that Santa came early to her house. Presents flooded the area under the tree and poured into the living room. All the female grandchildren would come over in nice dresses, with stockings, and fancy shoes. My grandfather owned a kosher deli, so we always had large spreads of meats, cheeses, and pickles. My aunt would make her famous veggie pizza, and other relatives would bring other appetizers and desserts. We would all gather and enjoy one another's company.

Gram was incredibly easy to shop for. When you saw a gift that reminded you of her and you could picture her laughing, you bought it. We opened gifts on Christmas Eve, after Gram had already consumed a few glasses of blush or white wine, with ice cubes. I do not think that was by mistake, as many of the gifts she would open would be inappropriate, hilarious, and would immediately go on her shelf, a nearby table, or whatever space was left for it to be seen. She filled her house, along with the help of her loved ones, with hilarious items that brought so much comfort and joy to be around. She had a ceramic dog that was in the lifted leg position. Anywhere she set it, the dog appeared to be relieving itself on that piece of furniture. Her house had always been filled with items such as these. In her kitchen she had plaques that read funny sayings. One I can recall read, "God doesn't want me and neither does the devil." She laughed so hard at that saying that when people would mention her age, she would recite that saying and cause everyone to laugh. Next to the nicest piece of china she owned would sit the most random or inappropriate clay figurine you have ever seen. Her decorating technique was a constant reminder not to take life too seriously, and to fill your home with items that make you laugh and bring you joy.

One year, at an art fair, my parents found a gift perfect for Gram on Christmas. The gift was a Jester face and hands were made of clay and body of fabric. He sat in her china cabinet for years, and had a sign that read, "gesture" while he held his clay middle finger up. Gram got such a kick out of this, that she put it on display for everyone to see. Another year, my cousin gave her a piece of oriental ceramic art. It was two pieces. The first clay piece was of a man bending over, the second was of a little girl lying on her stomach on the ground, pointing and laughing at the man's behind. These off color or unique gifts made her laugh so hard, and she would put them on display in her home for everyone's entertainment.

Gram always had a drink in hand on Christmas Eve. Usually it was poured from whatever bottle of wine was open, with ice cubes. She played this game every year where she would buy an object, one per family, wrap it for everyone, and then we would go around the room trying to guess what the purpose of the object was. I can recall a red device used for measuring pasta. All the adults were completely stumped. She never gave a context for the gift, so it could literally be used for any purpose. The guesses would always be hilarious and it was a matter of minutes into playing that the adults would be hysterically laughing, most would be in tears. Gram knowing the answer, of course, always got the biggest kick from watching the adults guess. She would let it go on for a long time before she would finally tell them. The last gift I can recall her giving like this was a few years back. She gave all the adults a framed picture of Chinese letters. No one in the family can read Chinese, so she finally told us that it read, "I am still here." She gave one to each family when she was at the age of ninety-three. She wanted to remind everyone to get off her back about eating right and working out. She said, "I've been doing what I have been doing my whole life and I am not going to change it now. I am still here, aren't I?" Everyone laughed out loud, and now we all have this hilarious reminder of Gram and her legacy continues to live on in all of us. She is still here.

Gram was just as playful as a grandmother as she was as a parent. The fond memories I have of sleepovers at such a young age will live on with me forever. I will always remember the simple situations she turned into magic. She knew how to turn an ordinary event into a playful activity. Overnights at Grandma's were always an exciting adventure! Usually we would be dropped off and then immediately pile in her car and go to Ben Franklin's, a candy store in Webster. This candy store was seriously every child's dream—rows and rows of candy from floor to ceiling. When my brother and I arrived at the store, Gram would hand us small baskets that we could fill as high as we would like with candy. After leaving with our large candy bags, we would head back to the house to play a game while Gram made us whatever we wanted for dinner. She was always focused on making the ones she loved happy.

More often than not, I would color with these awesome crayons Grandma had that looked like colored pencils. If I was not coloring, I was watching television, because Gram had cable and while growing up at my house, we did not. There were what felt like a million cartoon channels to watch on her TV. She would build what she referred to as a "nest" around our bodies with blankets and pillows, as we sat on the couch in her sunroom. I remember loving the "nests" she would build and feeling so comfortable in her place. About this time, the sun would be setting, I would be in another room away from Gram, and I would notice lights turning on without anyone touching any switches. Lights turning on and off by themselves is not the type of event that sits well with a young girl, especially this particular young girl that knew nothing of timers. "Grrrammm..." I would call out. When Gram would enter the room, I would inquire about the lights, and she would say it was her friendly ghost, "Max." She told me that he came around at dusk and turned the lights on for her.

A few things here: how on earth you tell a young child a "ghost" is turning lights on and off without scaring them, is beyond me, but she accomplished that. I asked her where Max lived in the house and she said the basement. I can recall curiously peering down the old wooden steps into the cement storage cellar. It was so dark and scary, filled with packing boxes and maybe a tiny window or two. The space itself was so terrifying that I absolutely believed a ghost lived down there. I trusted for years and years that Gram had a friendly ghost living in her home. I think she still would have convinced me of that well into adulthood, had my mother not told me the lights were actually on timers.

After the Max conversation, we would eat dinner that was usually made up of my favorite tortellini, Kosher salami, deli pickles, homemade Gooeybutter cake, and a popsicle. We ate well at Gram's, because she always had our favorite food. Dinner was followed by my most fond memory of Gram's growing up, bath time. She had the best bath toys. She had enough plastic food item toys that we could pretend to have our very own grocery store. She had fruits, veggies, all kinds of juices and milk cartons that all fit into a little drink basket. Gram would pretend like I was the storeowner selling the produce and would hand me fake money in exchange for these colorful grocery items. I loved this game because she did such a fantastic job playing along. She would enter the room each time as if she had never been to that store before, and after she purchased her apple and made small talk, she would exit. I would prepare for her next appearance after she left the room. Sometimes it would take longer for her to reenter, and one time I got out of the tub to find out where she had gone, to find her face nearly pressed up against her small bedroom television watching what appeared to be an extremely suspenseful moment in Wheel of Fortune.

It amazes me when I think about the simple situations, like her lights were actually on timers and when her grandchild asked her about the lights going on by themselves, instead of simply telling her they are on timers, she invented this imaginary ghost friend. I will never forget her saying that. It was such a playful delight, as a child, thinking a special, helpful "ghost" turned Gram's lights on and off. It actually became so significant and memorable that my brother, Ryan, and I voted to name our family dog, "Max." Gram had this way of turning a situation so simple into a playful concept or story that excited everyone involved. Her imagination was incredible.

On holidays and every other day in between, Gram was always able to find a way to add play into her daily routine. She seemed to do it effortlessly and with such grace. I remember moving into my own house. I was so wrapped up in "making it nice," for others to admire. I accepted anything and everything great aunts passed down to me, grandma passed down, my parents, and other family members. My house was a mess, and I was constantly switching out furniture for other furniture because maybe it was newer, or maybe it looked nicer, or was more expensive. Not until I began using my grandmother's approach to decorating did I became truly happy in my home. My place is filled with meaningful trinkets, artwork that I love, furniture I enjoy and I have never felt more at home and comfortable in my space surrounded by the things I enjoy. My style is playful and comfortable, and not for anyone else's approval but my own.

When I think of making time for play and how effortlessly my grandmother seemed to do this in her life, I realize examples such as how Mary Hoopefoodle came into being, Max the friendly ghost, and the stocking for "nobody" all involved a playful perspective on an ordinary situation. I am sure all mothers would agree, hearing "mom" repeated is annoying as hell, and all kids are guilty of it at one time or another. Most moms would also agree, at some point or another, they have experienced a mishap occurring for which none of their children will take ownership. I do not know of many homes using timers to the extent my grandmother did. However, I think we can agree some things happen that either we cannot explain, do not know how to explain, or because of their age can not completely explain to a child. The secret weapon my grandmother had in order to pull these ideas off was an incredible imagination.

I have found that as I age, it becomes more and more difficult to use my imagination. I do, however, believe it is absolutely crucial to living a life filled with joy. I have a hunch that with technological advances we rely less and less on our imagination because almost as soon as we have a question, we can answer it with the touch of a button. Since most of us carry these buttons that have all the answers to our questions, fully charged in our pockets and purses, less and less do we have need for our imagination.

As I work diligently at improving my imagination, I have found that spending time away from technology and around children is most helpful in nurturing this joy-producing tool. By no means have I mastered this art form; however, a few tricks I have learned while working to improve it is first letting go. Allowing myself to be goofy, and not concerned with what others may think around me has been most helpful. I have found it easiest to get in touch with my inner child and find time to play when I am around children, playing hide and seek, drawing with sidewalk chalk or playing with bubbles. I have even stocked the trunk of my car so that I am ready to play when an opportunity presents itself. I have bubble wands and bubble containers, a baseball glove and ball, tennis racket, and soccer ball in my trunk at all times. Because, why not? I can assure you carrying all of these toys around in my car, they have had much more use than if they were being stored in my basement or in the garage.

I learned from Gram that "playing" does not mean single player games on my phone. It involves human interaction, getting outside, enjoying the people around me, and letting go of potential judgment from those around me. Embracing life and living in the moment, doing what feels right for you, regardless of what others may think is all part of being able to play. Somewhere in my mid-twenties I forgot what making time for play was all about. It is interesting that as these devices we carry around become more and more essential we do less and less of what they were originally meant for, communicating. I have found that playing and imagination happen outside these electronic devices and when we are in the company of others. The smallest changes that have made the biggest impact for me in this category have been playing games with family and friends, filling my home and living space with items that bring me joy, and using my imagination to create and dream. The Life my grandmother led serves as a constant reminder to make time for play. She incorporated the use of her imagination into her parenting style, grandparenting style, everyday life, holidays, and she prided herself on having playful décor not for anyone else's approval but her own.

CHAPTER 3:

FOLLOW YOUR HEART AND IGNORE OUTSIDE VOICES

"Nope! I am afraid I will have to swim back."

My grandma's father left their family when Gram was a toddler. As a single mother, my great grandmother knew that society and others had many opinions on how she should behave in this situation. She was to move back in with her parents, and never date or marry again. Gram was too young to fully understand what was going on when they moved back in with her grandparents. Even as a child, she did not pay attention to the thoughts or opinions of society.

When my grandmother was growing up, society's views were not accepting and cruel. Blacks and whites were segregated, African Americans were believed to be inferior to white Americans and were therefore treated unjustly, segregated, forced to use separate gathering places, bathrooms, apartments were not rented to them and so many more unjust acts. White Americans treated black Americans cruelly as a result of the general public opinions. Others thoughts and opinions did not hold much weight with my grandmother, even as a child. She described to me how she would gravitate toward African Americans. Whether it be on the street, on the bus, any place she would see them, Gram was accepting and comfortable visiting with them.

At this time many different groups were looked down on by society. If you were a gay man or woman, society considered you an outcast as well. Many too afraid to live freely, married and wore a mask to society concealing their true identity. Homosexuality was believed to be by the choice of the individual, and completely against the beliefs of the church. Society did not view homosexuals as equal to heterosexual Americans, and many avoided contact with those who were openly gay. Gram told me that as a child living with her grandparents, there was a homosexual man that lived alone down the street. She described how her mother would make him a plate of food and Gram would bring it to him. I love that my grandmother learned to be accepting of others from her mother. They were trailblazers and incredible examples to those around them.

Growing up my great grandmother never said a negative thing about her husband who had abandoned her, not to my grandmother anyway. Gram did not hear from her father until she was about seven years old, and her father came back with the promise of an all girls' private school he could send her to up north. Her mother, knowing she could not afford such schooling for Gram, let her father take her to Pittsburgh. Once she arrived, Gram realized her father had lied to her mother. There was no "private girl's school." Instead, he had taken Gram to live with his wife and kids in Pittsburgh, and sent her to school across the street. She began writing her mother letters to tell her the truth and would give them to her father to mail. After a few letters and no response from her mother, my grandma knew her mom was not receiving her letters. At the young age of seven, she decided to write a new letter explaining everything and asked the school's cook to send it. It was not but a few days that passed before her mother was at the school in a cab to pick Gram up to take her back home to Saint Louis. The school had been instructed to immediately notify her father if anyone other than himself came to pick up my grandma. Sure enough by the time Gram and her mom made it to the train station, her father was standing on the platform waiting for them. Gram does not remember much about the conversation between her mother and father on that day. The only memory that remained was holding on to her mother so tightly and never wanting to let go. Sure enough, the pair traveled home that day to Saint Louis.

Her mother was fearless, strong and set an incredible example for my Gram. Society's views at this time were incredibly closed-minded. Those suffering with mental health issues were another group of individuals completely shunned at that time. Gram explained to me how there was a room at her elementary school for "special kids," and how her heart broke for those children so much so she was determined to bring these children happiness in some way. She described how she would stay inside and play with these children during her recess time, in hopes of bringing them joy.

My grandmother never allowed the opinions of society to dictate the words she spoke or the actions she made. I am so glad she insisted on following her heart because that is what led her to my grandpa. Gram was eighteen and went out with a girlfriend to hear a band play. My grandfather was an entertainer and singing that evening. He was almost two years older than Gram, and immediately attracted to her. She described him to me as, "Old for his age. He had seen a lot," she told me. He asked her out and the two dated. On their first date, grandpa took her to a "black and tan," after hours club. She said it was entirely different than anything she had ever experienced. The year was 1936, and blacks and whites were still segregated with the exception of special clubs. In her lifetime, as time continued, acceptance was beginning to occur among society and these groups. Blacks and whites slowly, over time, became integrated. In her late teens, when my grandmother met my grandfather, who was an entertainer, the two would go to "Black and Tan clubs," where both black and whites were welcomed. Gram was always incredibly open minded and accepting of all people. It was clear that as a child she saw no difference between herself and others regardless of their skin color, sexual preference, IQ, or anything else for that matter. The opinions of society have slowly shifted to what they are today, a place that is not perfect but much improved from where they were. What did not change was how Gram felt about the differences that make people, individuals. She always welcomed diversity and what made individuals unique.

One Valentine's Day, when they were dating, they went to see live entertainment. Gram told me, "He leaned over and whispered in her ear, 'Will you marry me'." She responded, "Let me think about it," because she was so surprised. After grandpa asked Gram to marry him, she told her mother the news. Her mother was concerned about the fact that grandpa was Jewish. Outsiders had discouraged my grandmother from dating grandpa because he carried two unpopular titles with society. For one, he was an entertainer. It was believed then that you do not date an entertainer, because there was considered to be no money in that industry. The second unpopular title was the fact that my grandfather had been raised Jewish. His name at birth was Jack Goldberg, but because he was Jewish, he thought he would never be hired in his industry, so he changed his name to Jackie Gold. The fact that Gram was Catholic and grandpa was Jewish presented an issue, because at that time it was not popular or common to marry outside your religion.

From an early age, my grandmother was never going to be told whom she would be allowed to talk to or what she was allowed to say. As she grew up, none of that changed and she definitely was not going to be told whom she could date or marry.

Gram's concerned mother decided to consult with the priest about the destiny of her Catholic daughter who was going against the church and marrying a Jewish man. The priest looked at my great grandmother, smiled, and said, "Well, she will never go hungry." That was all he said on the matter and with that my great grandmother felt comfortable in giving her daughter and future son-in-law her blessing. My grandparents were married by the Justice of the Peace in 1938; his brother stood by him and my grandmother's mother by her. I promise you, you have never heard of a man who loved a woman more than my grandfather loved my grandmother. He took such incredible care of her. She never did any shopping of any kind. Grandpa would even purchase all Gram's feminine products for her.

As time passed and Gram looked back on the events with her father as a child, she realized by modern day measures her father had actually kidnapped her. Her father would pop in about every six or so years with a crazy vacation idea or some empty promise. The older Gram grew the less interested she became in having anything to do with him. When my grandparents were dating her dad showed back up to ask Gram to accompany him on a trip to Africa. Her reply to his inquiry was, "Nope! I am afraid I will have to swim back." She made it clear to him that she did not trust him. Early in their married life, my grandparents were invited to a cousin's wedding. This was the next time she heard from him, he had come in to give his sister's daughter away. My grandparents and great grandmother attended the wedding together. He mentioned that he was giving her cousin away at the wedding and Gram said, "You are good at giving kids away." She had no problem articulating exactly how she felt.

I love her fearless spirit, and how she said exactly what was on her mind. Her father felt foolish after she made such a humbling remark to him and followed it up with, "Come on now, let me get you a drink." And with that, my grandfather shot up out of his chair and sternly looked her father in the eyes and said, "If she needs anything at all, I will get it for her." She explained to me, when telling me this story, that it was grandpa's way of saying "back off." Anything she wanted or needed, grandpa provided. I am so glad she followed her heart and ignored the opinions of others because listening to her heart and marrying him brought them both so much joy.

Even when grandpa was off at war, he made sure she was cared for. Gram moved into a new apartment after he was drafted into WWII. They had just moved out of a two family flat and she had a bill of sale that granted her the rights to a piece of a furnace that was inside their old place. She had notified the new owners and they were refusing to return her calls or let her in to get the item that was rightfully hers. She believed they were doing this because the item itself was not inexpensive. Gram finally went to grandpa's lawyer and the lawyer sent a man to meet Gram at her old place. The new owners were inside and not responding to Gram's knocking. The short Italian man the lawyer had sent, looked at my grandmother and said, "Jackie Gold?" to which she replied, "Yes." "Is that your husband?" Gram replied, "Yes." And with that the man said, "Okay!" He walked over to the door handle and he looked at my grandma and said, "I can't count to ten, I can only count to three. I am shooting the door open." When she told me this story I looked at her shocked and said, "Wait, Gram, what?" and she laughed and said, "Yep and, by God, that was the kind of lawyer we had." She went on to explain that the men knew my grandfather, and that was not the type of thing anyone would get away with doing to Jackie Gold. That man shot the door handle off, and sure enough, Gram retrieved the property that was rightfully hers.

While he was in the war, grandpa wrote to her everyday for three years. Gram said she did not keep the letters, because once he came home they wanted to forget he had been away and the war that had kept them apart. He was so loyal to her and loved her so much that it was even important to him that her mother be cared for properly, for that reason Grams' mother moved in with them. Gram explained to me, "My husband wanted my mom living with us. How many do that?" It was clear my grandmother loved that about my grandfather. It meant so much to her that he understood and respected her mother so much.

My grandpa had the right kind of friends and knew the kind of people you wanted to know back then. He loved my grandma so much and would do absolutely anything he could to keep her safe and protected. Grandpa owned a few nightclubs and Gram explained that she rarely went into them because grandpa was so protective of her. One night, she was picking him up from work for some reason and she took a seat at the bar. Well, a man came and sat next to Gram and grandpa was not amused. She explained to me that the poor man was not even talking to her, but it did not matter to my grandfather. He came over and picked that man and his barstool up in the air and moved him further away from my Gram. He made sure there was not a shadow of a doubt in anyone's mind that Gram was his wife.

Being in the entertainment industry my grandmother explained to me that my grandfather met a lot of people. "Good and bad people, none were bad for him. But for someone else they could be a little Mafia," she explained to me. During one of our long conversations she described to me another night she had accompanied grandpa out on the town. Apparently, some man had been looking at Gram in a way grandpa did not approve of, so, in her words, he "knocked the shit out of him." She went on to tell me that the man went on to put a "price" on my grandfather's head. Once the mafia got wind that there was a price on his head, they responded that they "did not want a hair on his head hurt." Gram told me, "With that, the price was immediately removed." Grandpa knew the right people to make sure he would be taken care of, and more importantly to him, so would my grandmother. Grandpa stood up for her and took care of her, and she loved him for that.

When Gram and grandpa married and began having children, the expectation of women had not shifted much from when Gram was growing up. It was still expected that the woman stay at home with the children, take care of the home, handle all chores, cook, all while remaining well maintained, polite, without voicing many opinions. Society's expectations of ladies were never something Gram paid much attention to. She always said what was on her mind. If people did not like what she was saying, it did not faze her or change her opinion.

One of the favorite stories Gram would tell me growing up, exemplified this beautifully. My grandmother was outside gardening on a gorgeous day in Saint Louis. She was in the front yard and had placed a playpen outside near her where her two infants were playing. As she was gardening, the little boy from next door had dragged the hose from his house over. The water from his hose was on and he was spraying the playpen and Gram's little ones inside. She asked him to stop a few times, but he continued to spray the boys. Finally, she ripped the hose from his hands and said "If you don't stop squirting my boys I am going to shove this hose where the sun don't shine." Not missing a beat the little boy looked up at her and said, "And just how are you going to do that." She was so frustrated by his wise remark and once that became apparent to him through her facial expression, the little boy ran off.

Hours later, Gram was inside making dinner when she heard a knock at the door. She opened it to find the boy's grandmother and mother standing at the door waiting for an explanation of what Gram had said to the little boy. Gram never held back from saying what she wanted to say. She never would have held back simply because it was something "women" should not say, think, express, according to social norms. She always said what was on her mind. She said the things most people only thought, because she did not care what others opinions were of her. She never stopped being herself for fear of being judged, which I think contributed to her overall happiness. She said what she felt regardless of the opinions of whoever was listening.

My grandmother was vocal about her feelings. She did not allow herself to get walked on. She stood up for what she believed was right. One day she received notice that my dad had been drafted for Vietnam. Her oldest son was in Vietnam already and had written her second son, my dad, and said, "If you go to war, go to Canada, do not let them send you over here." Gram did not think it was right that two of her sons would have to go so she wrote to the congressman and said, "I have one son there already, I do not think I should have two." She told me that by return mail, my dad had been taken off the list. She reflected to me about the wars she had experienced in her lifetime and thought it was all such a shame. Her father fought in WWI, her husband in WWII, and she had a son fight in Vietnam. While my dad served in the army reserves he was never drafted, thanks to Gram's letter. I am so grateful she stood her ground and voiced her opinion.

After her boys grew up and moved out, my grandparents continued to live in the castle house. Gram shared a story with me about one time when avid churchgoers were making the rounds to collect money from people in the neighborhood for the church. They came to her door in pairs and were all really friendly. Their house was technically in three parishes, she explained to me that there was one day where it was one after another ringing the bell. Finally after the third ring of the doorbell, my grandfather said, "Let me handle this one." Gram described how, "He opened the door with a Jewish accent." She chuckled, "And you have never heard anything more funny in your life." She described how these two nice men continued talking to my grandfather, although the looks on their faces were of obvious confusion and finally my grandfather said, "You know what, I will give you my saloon, and I will take the church." She laughed so hard telling me that story and after finally catching her breath described how the men walked away with expressions of "Who was he and what the hell were we doing there?" She laughed and said how badly she had wished tapes or recordings had existed in the capacity they do today. She would have loved to have been able to play that conversation back. Gram truly thought the world of how well he treated and cared for her. She also got the biggest kick out of him and his sense of humor. They really enjoyed one another's company.

My grandmother was truly the happiest person I have ever met. When I think about the common themes that exist in the stories she would tell me they were that of following her heart, intuition, and gut. The theme of ignoring the opinions of everyone else around her was one of my favorite themes. I think I enjoy it mostly because society has shifted so much in the direction of acceptance, that she had been practicing and stuck true to all those years. I love the stories of her fearlessness and standing up for herself. One hilarious story my oldest cousin shared with me describes Gram to a tee. On a nice day in Saint Louis, my cousin was driving around with a bunch of his guy friends just after he had turned sixteen. On their joy ride the guys noticed a black Audi and the license plate read "2GOLD." Grandpa had personalized plates made for his car and hers. His plate read "1GOLD" and hers "2GOLD"; so adorable. Nonetheless, the boys knew right away it was Gram because of her plates. They all thought it was a riot that it was Aaron's grandma so they began honking the horn to get her attention. Gram had no idea it was Aaron and his friends and instead figured someone was disagreeing with her driving ability. All of a sudden the sunroof opens and Aaron and his friends witness Gram's middle finger, flicking them off, out of her sunroof. I spoke earlier of how Gram gave people her middle finger when they did not agree with her view or stance on things; well, there you have it. She just did not care what other people thought of her. She was going to be who she was and do what she wanted regardless.

Her views and actions were opposite of society and she was right. Ultimately, social norms and opinions would change over time to meet Gram's views. She remained true to how she felt and what she knew to be just regardless of others opinions. As a result of following her heart and ignoring the opinions of others, she married an incredible man who absolutely adored her. He saw to it that she was always cared for and safe. The two lived a life of laughter and enjoyed one another's company. She lived a life of inclusiveness, accepting all kinds of people, regardless of their skin color, sexual preference, or IQ and as a result her life was made richer. She never held back her thoughts or feelings for the sake of the opinions of others and for that reason we have many hilarious stories and lessons to live by. She blazed the trail for women so that we could clearly see the most efficient route to optimal happiness.

I have found, as time progresses and technology improves, it has become more and more of a challenge to get in touch with my gut feelings. It has become so incredibly easy to text a friend two pictures of outfits and ask, "Which should I wear?" It is too simple to gain the opinions of others or of the outside world. I am guilty of consulting people I do not even know via Trip Advisor or other websites to sway my opinion of which hotel to book. These may be simple, everyday examples, but when I think about big decisions I have made, I think about all the people I consult before making that decision. And for what reason? Why would I allow anyone to sway my opinions or decisions? I think about the pressure I have felt from society throughout my life, the opinions of "everybody," none of which I can individually name. I believe it is nearly impossible not be influenced by social norms. It is definitely the safer option, to stay within the expectations of society and others. No one will look at you, you will not stand out, you will not be a topic of conversation, and it is definitely the safest way to live. You will be much less likely to be criticized, noticed, or pointed out. Since this book is not about telling you the safest solutions on how to live your life but is instead, a guide to living a life filled with more joy, we must now consider this question: will living a life within the boundaries and expectations of society and others make you the most joyful, happy individual you can be? With the life my grandmother lived as a guide, I would have to answer, absolutely not. Playing it safe does not equate to optimal joy. The opinions of society shift and change as time goes on, along with the opinions of those around us as they age. Following your heart, gut, voice, whichever you prefer to call it, is absolutely the quickest way to achieve happiness and optimal joy.

Need help getting in touch with
your gut feelings?

Visit **www.StephGoldLifeCoach.com**
to schedule a complimentary
phone consultation

CHAPTER 4:
OPEN DOOR POLICY

"I had four boys. My house sounded like a zipper factory in the morning"

One of the lessons from the life of my grandmother that resonated possibly the loudest for me is that of her open door policy. Throughout her life she was constantly welcoming in people and animals alike. She taught me through her stories and example that the universe constantly offers each one of us gifts and if we accept them with open arms the result will be joy. Often in the moment it may seem like a lot of work or too much effort to take in someone or an animal that needs a home. It is easier to kindly refuse to be inconvenienced by the hassle and stress of taking care or lending a hand to someone in need, even if only for a short period of time.

Of course, few people truly have the space to house another human being. My grandmother never saw taking someone in as an inconvenience. She did not view it as an option. She constantly said yes to people and had an open invitation to any friend or relative that wanted or needed a place to stay. I have described how she had four boys and how her husband insisted that Gram's mother live with them. Her home was cozy. The main floor had a small living room, a narrow sunroom off the living room, a cozy dining room, kitchen, small laundry room that led to an unfinished basement they used as storage, a tiny half bath, and small entryway. Up her spiral staircase was a master bedroom, two small bedrooms, and one full bath at the end of the hallway. Many would see her home and think, how on earth did seven people live in this home, let alone have an inch of space for another human being. When Gram would tell stories she would say, "There was always a fifth boy, someone else was always living with us." Usually, it was a friend of one of her boys. Some guests would only stay for a night, many stayed longer, weeks even months. Friends always knew they were welcome at Grams for as long as they wanted or needed.

One year, early in their marriage, my grandfather brought a stripper to Christmas Eve dinner. Being in the entertainment industry, grandpa had brought the stripper to the Veterans' show, and afterward he told Gram she was coming over for Christmas Eve dinner. Gram did not mind, of course. She did not have a judgmental bone in her body. Gram explained to me how they could not strip all the way down in those days. She described how she had one uncle at dinner who was having the time of his life after the stripper walked in. She did not strip at Gram's house of course; she was just there to enjoy dinner.

Gram loved people, but that was not all she welcomed freely into her home. My grandmother had a serious love for animals. Her love ran so deep that the local Humane Society would call her before putting down a dog. That was how she ended up with a standard poodle. She was driving a convertible at the time and described to me how she had to put the roof down for the dog to fit inside. If an animal needed a home, Gram went to his or her rescue! Joe Russo was an entertainer my grandfather knew. When he and his wife got a divorce, they left their tan collie in their yard. Gram got wind of this and she put my father in the car and went over to save the dog. The two drove to the Russo's and my Gram sent my father to retrieve the dog from the yard. She told me, "Of course the dog puked all the way home. It had developed a tic, from being nervous. It took a long time for the tic to go away, but it was a wonderful dog." She went on to describe how later on, "Joe Russo came to see me and Jack one time, when Jay was a baby in the playpen. Joe went over to my third child and that dog would not let him, even though it remembered him. The dog did not bite, but it pushed Joe away from the baby." The animals Gram took in were so incredibly loved by her that they were extremely loyal. Neighbors used to say, "you get the darndest pets. They never leave your yard".

Gram absolutely adored animals and was ready to give a home to any in need. One Easter morning, my grandfather came home with two little ducks. They were the sweetest little things. Gram and Grandpa stacked tires up in the back yard and made a safe little home for the ducks. Only one of the ducks survived but their young boys loved that sweet little thing. They named the duck Marilyn because when she walked she would shake her tail from side to side. The way she walked reminded my grandmother of Marilyn Monroe. Gram described how she, "Grew up and never left the yard. The duck stayed with the kids." The neighborhood had a dog parade and the boys dressed up the duck. They walked in the parade but then the duck's feet became hot from walking on the black top and my dad ended up carrying the poor thing the rest of the way. Marilyn had quite the personality. Gram described how she would make so much noise. She would wake up the neighborhood when the sun was rising. Gram said, "She even made noise at night. When we were at the neighbor's house, Marilyn told us when it was time to go home." Finally, the noise became too much to bear and they needed to find a new home for Marilyn. Gram said, "My cousin's husband said he would let it loose in the park, which he did, and I felt bad about it." Then, the craziest thing happened. Her face lit up when she told me that, "Three days later there was a picture in the paper about a duck that followed people into the Muny Opera." Her cousin's husband had let Marilyn go at the pond just outside the Muny. The news just tickled Gram to read that in the paper because she knew it just had to be Marilyn. "All she knew was people," Gram would say.

Grandma had animals with personality and the stories she would share were absolutely hilarious. She had a cat once that came inside dragging something. When she came closer to see what it was the cat had, she realized it was a snake. The cat pulled the carpet up and had shoved the snake under it. Gram thought it was a riot, that is, once the snake had been removed from her home. The cat story that I found the most humorous was the cat that would go out the second story window and climb down the tree to go to the bathroom. My grandma would tell me how she thought this was the smartest cat in the world. She would leave the upstairs window cracked and the cat would climb down the tree and go outside. She explained how she watched the cat do this numerous times and thought the cat was incredibly smart. Yes, the smartest cat that ever lived, that is until she caught one of her boys sneaking out at night from the very same window. It was then that she realized that cat had watched her boys sneak out the window and climb down the tree and this cat had just followed their lead. I asked her to tell me that story again and again because she would laugh so hard when telling it to me. The part that made her laugh the most was the moment she realized the cat was not as intelligent as she had given him credit for.

In the 26 years I was able to spend with my grandma, I can recall a cat named Chastity, a small dog named Charlie, a Shih Tzu called Irish, a Lhasa Apso named Mercedes, another Lhasa Apso named Lexus, and birds. I think she was only watching the birds while my Uncle and Aunt were out of town, but they made an impression on me still. For only six years of my life I did not have a family pet, and it traumatized me. Those six years overshadow the other twenty-two years I have lived with animals, so going to Gram's and seeing all types of pets, including birds, made a lasting impression.

Grams open door policy applied to animals and people alike, when raising her four boys, they would always have at least one extra friend living at the house. She jokingly described how her house sounded life a "zipper factory" in the morning when all the boys were getting ready for school. Often when other boys were staying at her home, their stay would overlap holidays. Her holidays were open to anyone who needed a warm house to come to or wanted one that was guaranteed to be filled with laughter and celebration. One Christmas, when her boys were teenagers, she had an extra boy at the house and she wanted to be sure he had something to open Christmas morning while her boys opened their gifts. When she asked him what he wanted, he told her he wanted a wetsuit. Gram was at such a loss. Living in the middle of the country, not near any large body of water, I cannot imagine these were easy to come by in the 50's and 60's. When she finally found one, the price was more than she was able to spend on her own boys. At a loss on what to do, she decided to wrap a box of condoms. Christmas morning the boy opened the box and turned to Gram, her reply, "That was the only rubber suit I could afford." Everyone laughed at her clever joke and she continued to tell that story for years to come.

My grandmother was always inviting people to stay with her, even after her children were grown. Once on a cruise, during their retirement, my grandfather and grandmother met a young German couple and their daughter. The family was having a hard time communicating their order to the wait staff on the ship and my grandfather overheard and walked over to help them. Grandpa remembered some German from being in the war. Gram explained to me that, "He was in Germany a long time and was there at the end of the war. He could speak Yiddish, which meant he could kind of understand German and could talk to prisoners. At some point he acted as an interpreter." The German family was so relieved that someone could help them communicate that they were glued to my grandfather's hip for the rest of the trip. After the cruise was over and they were all at the airport, saying "goodbye" to their new friends, my grandmother made a comment that they should come visit them in Saint Louis and stay with her someday. There may have been a slight misunderstanding or language barrier, but regardless with that the family walked up to the check in counter and immediately had their flights changed. They got on Gram and Grandpa's flight home and came to stay at their house, right then and there. Stories like this were an everyday occurrence in Gram's life; she was constantly taking people in to stay with her.

Gram loved the holidays and she never turned down a soul who wanted to celebrate with her. A few of my uncles divorced yet Gram continued to include both of their ex-wives and then later their ex-wives boyfriends to be a part of her celebration. I realize now, looking back, that may not always work and I am sure people had their differences and issues, but you would never have known because Gram's home was a place of love and acceptance and all those attending just seemed to get along. She never turned down anyone that needed a place to go. She always held a Christmas Eve celebration and would have a gift for everyone.

If someone wanted to stay with her, he or she was always welcome the reason never mattered to Gram. Maybe you are thinking sure, what is one more boy when you already have four, but she continued to live by this rule throughout her entire life. After my grandfather passed away, in her seventies and eighties Gram took in both of her youngest sons who were both ill. She cared for them for years until they passed. In her early eighties, she took in three of my cousins who had lost their mother and father. Gram cared for these three girls and was essentially raising three teenagers in her eighties. She never missed a beat and was happy to take them in. She never made it seem like her life was inconvenienced in anyway, always taking in others. Gram would tell stories of how much richer her life was for these experiences.

The people and animals my grandmother welcomed into her life with open arms made her life more enjoyable. When you offer your home to a soul who is in need of a home, he or she is forever grateful. I believe this is why the animals and people she rescued were so loyal to her and insanely protective. I believe it also to be the reason why people extended their stay or returned regularly. The comfort of her hospitality was reassuring and encouraging to those experiencing tough times. She had a way of making others feel at ease and take comfort in knowing everything was going to work out and while in limbo why not have a few laughs? To go from the fear of not knowing where your next meal will come from, where you will sleep, or how you will be cared for and then to be welcomed by a joyful and hilarious woman who just makes all the details of life seem effortless, it is no wonder animals never left and people returned time and time again. Her welcoming spirit made others feel so comfortable that they continued to gravitate toward her no matter the circumstance.

CHAPTER 5:
MAKE IT POSITIVE

"God doesn't want me and the devil doesn't either."

When my uncle Jay, Gram's third child, was a toddler he watched as his older brothers walked off to school every morning. One day he and his neighborhood playmate decided they too wanted to walk to school like their older siblings. Gram had a baby at home, her youngest, my uncle Jim. She was preoccupied with him and did not notice that Jay, the neighbor girl, and their Collie were walking to school. Once they arrived at school, the dog would not allow any of the school's staff to come near these two children. The teachers and other staff members were at a loss on what to do. They did not know who the parents of these two little children were. Finally, the school got in touch with the police. But once the police arrived, the dog would not allow the policemen near the children. Finally, the adults discovered which household the children belonged to and the police were somehow able to allure the dog and children into the patrol car. My young and mischievous uncle somehow disconnected the officer's radio once in the vehicle, and the police drove around and around until finally finding my grandmother's place.

Gram would tell me this story when we spoke about all the pets she had. She would say, "Collies are the smartest dogs I ever owned." She loved that the dog kept her little guy safe. She would laugh and laugh talking about how Jay turned the radio off, how the kids walked to school before they were old enough to even attend. It was a light hearted story about how these two little ones wanted to go to school like their older siblings. As an adult, what absolutely amazes me is that she did not mention all of the stress and concern that went along with this event. I can only imagine the fear and concern one would experience after realizing her four year old is missing. How scary it would be to see a police car drive up to your house with your child inside. Of course, my grandma had to have felt all these emotions but the way she chose to tell the events from that day made it a light hearted, enjoyable story about two adventurous kids and a heroic dog. This story remains one of my all time favorites that my grandmother would tell me. It serves as the perfect example of how Gram's decision to focus on the positive played out in her life.

One morning, Gram was cooking breakfast. She had her boys and her usual couple others. The boys were sitting in her breakfast window and shouting out their orders. My father was an extremely picky eater and had changed his order multiple times. "Finally, after about the tenth change, I took an egg and threw it at him," she told me. It landed in the center of his forehead and the yolk ran down his face. Of course, everyone burst out laughing. It absolutely amazes me how in that moment when even the most patient person would become annoyed or frustrated, Gram found a way to focus on what mattered and stay positive by making everyone laugh.

My grandmother's ability to see the positive in situations was unbelievable. Having as many children as she did offered the opportunity for more excitement in life. The fact that all four were boys makes life even more interesting. Gram told me, "We had a neighbor that complained about my kids. He did not like how they were cutting through his yard and killing his grass." Remember the time and social norm when my grandmother was raising her boys. There were certain expectations of women at this time. Even now if a neighbor approached me about a situation like this I do not know that my first inclination would not be to speak to my children. Get mad, raise my voice, sounds negative, and I am sure my approach would not be effective and instead upset my children and myself. My grandmothers' response to this angry neighbor was this, "You either have good kids and half-assed grass, or half-assed kids and good grass." She later found out this man broke out in hives over her response, which I find hilarious. This situation could have very easily ended negatively but, instead my Gram took it as an opportunity to remain positive and basically tell this over stuffed old man to relax and focus on the things in life that matter. I am sure he thought telling my grandmother about the issue would take care of it and had no idea she would basically throw it back in his face and tell him she did not care about his grass. I do not know what came of that man but I am sure he got over it, no one stayed mad at Gram; she was too much of a joy to be around. My grandmother had a way of turning a situation that would usually be frustrating into laughter. She had a way of remaining grounded about what was important in life and not allowing herself to focus on the negative.

When my father was a junior in high school, a group of his friends decided they wanted to do a junior prank. It was customary for the seniors to prank the school, but his group of friends did not want to wait another year. The boys came up with an amazing idea. They told college friends to drop off beer cans at my grandmother's house. Boys would drive by and leave large trash bags of beer cans on the lawn. Dad and his friends stored them in Gram's garage. After months of collecting hundreds of cans, the boys started stringing all the cans together. Gram told me that she noticed all these cans being dropped off and she thought it was odd, but did not really ask any questions. One night the guys snuck out and took all these ropes of cans up to the school. Gram said, "What they did was decorate the trees outside the high school with beer cans. And every beer can was placed perfectly." Cans covered the trees, flagpole, bushes, the grounds were beautifully decorated with strings of beer cans. My grandmother was called up to school by the head of school. When she arrived, she was amazed. She described the scene to me, "There were thousands of beer cans. They were all strung together, decorating the outside of school. Rick was a junior when he did this. They had to take down every can, or else we had to pay one hundred and fifty dollars for someone else to do it. But the boys took it down, and they did a beautiful job." My dad said that the junior's prank was so incredible that the seniors were furious that no one would remember whatever prank they pulled that year. My dad and his friends were so proud of themselves for pulling this off and to this day that prank is a legend at the High School.

I find it amazing that all Gram could say was "They had done a beautiful job". She was truly impressed with the boys. I think that is so neat that she was able to see this prank as a positive story. So many parents would have gotten upset, grounded the kids, or made it a negative story about the day my father defaced school property and completely went against the law. No one was hurt and no property was harmed. They were called into school and they cleaned it all up. There was no need for this situation to have been made a bigger deal than necessary. I love that Gram was able to be so positive about a situation that most would have seen as negative.

After her boys grew up and moved out, my Grandparents bought a place in Lake Saint Louis. When they were living in the "castle house" in Webster, they also had a place at the lake. When describing it Gram said, "When you are in business for yourself, you never take vacations. The condo was like a vacation on the weekends. We were right on the water." My Gram told me that my grandfather bought a pontoon boat. She said his intention was to have a "party boat." She said, "It did not last long with the boat. Jews do not make good sailors." She described how each time he tried to park the boat he would "take the dock with him each time. You know, he would forget to untie the rope." Finally, a neighbor said to him, "Jack, get rid of that. We'll take you anywhere you want to go on the lake." She said he had no idea how to turn the boat, but he thought it was great. I loved listening to her speak of my grandfather with such love. She never seemed to get worked up. I can imagine it would be slightly stressful having a husband who is upsetting the neighbors with his clear lack of experience operating this boat but she did not seem to mind, whatever made him happy. It is so refreshing to tell these stories and have the opportunity to sit back and reflect on just how incredibly positive she was about situations that arose throughout her lifetime.

I will forever remember one of our phone conversations while I was in college. Gram's eyesight was starting to deteriorate and she had just left one of her many eye doctor's appointments. I asked her how everything went and what the doctor said and she replied with a story. The doctor did not have many good things to say so Gram walked outside and sat on a bench while she waited for my Uncle Terry to bring around the car. As she rested there on a bench with plastic circular covers taped to her eyes, to protect them from the sunlight while being dilated, she sat and she looked around. She described how she would have to close one eye, and squint with the other to see what was around her through one of the holes. She described the most gorgeous street with shops and restaurants, with lampposts and park benches. "And Stephy," she said, "I think there are apartments above all of this that you would just love." She was describing the Boulevard in Brentwood, and when I reflect on this story in particular, I think about how many people would have enjoyed this experience...and realize not many. I did not hear about what the doctor said, how crushed she was that she was told she was not going to be able to see many of the things she enjoyed much longer. Instead I heard about the beauty around her. She described the most incredible street this office was located on. I do not know many people that would not have sat there contemplating the awful news, waiting in misery, unable to see, with uncomfortable hard covers taped to their eyes. But Gram chose not to see the cover as something restricting her vision instead she saw the covers as providing her a tiny little hole in which to see a magical little street. She had an incredible ability to find the positive in a situation and direct her attention there.

The magical little street she spoke of is across the street from the Saint Louis Galleria. It is less than a block from a noisy highway. The street stretches about one block; it contains a few shops and a PF Chang's. The lampposts are sweet and it does wind around. The apartments back up to the highway, which I would assume would be pretty annoying. I am not trying to be negative, but I do want to point out some of the details left out in Gram's story, because it is important to understand how natural this ability came for her. Over the years she had trained her brain to only see the positive in situations and only tell stories from that point of view. She had an incredible gift and I feel blessed to have witnessed it and her joy.

When Gram would comment on her age or question why she was still living a fairly healthy life, with a sharp memory and mind, she would usually include the quote, "God doesn't want me and the devil doesn't either." It was her way of joking around about the fact that she had lived so long. The friends and family she said this to would laugh when she gave her explanation for still being on earth. My grandma had a fabulous way of seeing the positive in situations. The truth is, it was never obvious that she was completely omitting the negative side of things, or the hardship involved. In other words, she would tell a story, you would listen and think, what an amazing time she had, what a great life she lived, and then you would think about the details of the event and realize that to most others telling that story it would have sounded very different.

I never heard her complain. She was constantly taking people in and caring for them. My grandfather was ill and she cared for him until he passed. Two of her sons lived with her when they were ill and she took care of both of them until they passed. One of my uncles would have seizures at the house while Gram was there. I can only imagine how hard that would have been on a woman her age. She would have been in her late 70s and early 80s. I find it amazing that she never complained or spoke of how difficult that was for her. She was truly happy caring for others and when asked about taking care of her sons she said, "I was happy to have them and just glad Jack was not there to see them sick like that."

Her way of viewing events in life was magical and inspiring. She truly had a gift. I know it to be one of the many reasons people would want to sit and talk to her for hours on end. She had such an amazing way of viewing the world and the common events that occur day to day. Even her mailmen would come inside and sit down to talk with her, each day when delivering her mail. My uncle, Terry, has the same mailman as my grandmother did years ago. Uncle Terry has told me of how this mailman will tell him each time he sees him of how much he enjoyed conversing with my Gram and misses her. Her positive outlook on life and ability to insert laughter was an absolute joy to every individual she encountered.

The stories my grandmother shared with me, were happy stories because of her perspective. She had such an incredible way of looking at life that is so inspiring. In order to witness or notice the things she did, she was always present, patient, and attentive to her surroundings. One could easily argue in a small home with four boys, there was never anytime or room for anything or anyone else. Gram always made time. She created space and allowed herself to be "inconvenienced" by the needs of others. As you look to "find the laugh" try not to become caught up in the details of life and take life's details too seriously. I must remind myself that traffic is not a reason to become frustrated. While sitting in traffic now, I remind myself to take a moment to remember how grateful I am that I have a car, arms to steer it, legs to drive it, eyes to see the road, etc. Wherever I am headed can wait a little longer while I listen to words of the music playing or turn off the music completely and notice the cars around, the people inside them, the trees, listen to the birds, or notice the scenery. More often than not I notice something hilarious and it serves as a humorous story to be shared when I finally do arrive at my destination.

I try not to get upset with the situations that are completely out of my control, like traffic, lines at the checkout counter, comments other people make, the weather, or flight delays. When I feel frustration kicking in I immediately search for the humor in the situation, the way Gram taught me. Making time for play is something I intentionally insert into a daily routine. Simple adventures like making a random trip to the store and purchasing a hula hoop and then attempting to hoop while watching television that evening or making it a point to lay in the hammock whenever I take my dog outside. Inserting play is so essential to finding joy. I remind myself that play not only involves letting go but also is most easily found in human interaction. While I do not have children of my own, I do find time to borrow my cousin's son for overnights, trips to Six Flags, and other fun outings. I also find time to play with children from other families and friends consistently because, as Gram displayed, it keeps us young and allows us to remember the pure joy of playing.

Following my heart and ignoring outside voices has been key to accomplishing my goals in life. People say all kinds of things and then change their minds. Ultimately, know no one else can make you happy or give you happiness; understand it must come from inside you. Following your heart is absolutely crucial to sustaining a life of optimal joy. Being vocal and standing up for oneself can be incredibly difficult yet freeing. This year I have paid extra attention to the direction my heart is guiding me. I will say a lot of changes have occurred in my life. Many relationships have shifted. I ended my time as a nanny forever, walking away from a consistent paycheck, to pursue my dreams. My life today-who I speak to daily, my living situation, how I spend each day working-all looks differently than it did a year ago. For me, it has been important to recognize that it is never too late to listen to my gut. Maybe you have known or had an idea that you should make a change for a while but today you finally found the courage. Trust yourself and know that any decision that is guided by your heart will not steer you wrong. It took a lot of strength and listening to my gut to get to where I am and it was not easy. As difficult as it was to make these changes, I must admit I have never felt more on track.

What I am suggesting is that to live a life of optimal joy you must listen to the voice inside you, guiding you. If you have a friendship that never feels quite even and never truly feels honest or real, listen. Be mindful that where you are putting energy you should always be receiving energy in return. Friendship requires contributions from both parties in order to have balance. If everyday you are doing something that makes you want to hit the snooze button eight more times or ultimately, is not heading you in the direction of your true life passion, listen. Life is too short not to live a life filled with joy. Make sure you are passionate about the work you are doing. I have realized by following these steps laid out for me by my Gram, the happiest woman I have ever met, that in order to be the most joyful, sometimes you have to eliminate the things or people causing you to feel discomfort. Ultimately, you must realize that joy is a choice.

This was the year I finally had an opportunity to follow Gram's lead by being "inconvenienced" by someone in need. I had just concluded my Life Coach training when a friend called me about what sounded like another nanny job. Ready to turn down the offer completely, my friend explained how the mother of this family was terminally ill and her family needed assistance. My dad had been ill for eight years at the time of this call and my heart broke for the children of this family. I accepted the job. I promised the father that once his wife passed, I would help his family get on their feet and would then continue on with my professional goals after he found someone more permanent for the position. This was an extremely challenging position given all the changes and emotions that were going on for this family. I had 18 years of experience with children, and eight years of experience with the cancer center at the hospital and coping with a parent's illness. When my replacement arrived, she was 20 years old. She had little to no experience with children, and she had zero experience with the effects of cancer, or knowledge of what these little ones had witnessed over the last year. She was walking into a beyond difficult situation, and was not prepared. I reached out to her in the case that she would want a friend or mentor that had previously worked with the family and needed any help adjusting. Within a month, I received a call. She was leaving the position with the family and needed a place to stay. I transformed my dining room into a bedroom. Within six hours, I had a Swedish au pair living in my dining room. She would remain my new roommate for a little over two weeks and I would aid her in finding a new job.

My sweet Swedish friend, was placed with a family in California where she stayed for the remainder of her time in The States. The family took a trip to Kansas City and I went to visit her. Months later, she took a road trip before heading back to Sweden and stayed with me in Arizona. We will be life long friends. She thanked me endlessly for what I had done for her. The amount of love and kindness someone in need of a place to stay will show you is absolutely indescribable. I learned quickly why Gram did this so often. The outpouring of love and gratitude you will receive in return for your small gesture is completely life changing and incredibly rewarding.

Turning a seemingly negative situation into a positive and uplifting story, I believe to be a true art form. It is not an easy task to turn a doctor's visit into a magical fairytale the way my grandmother did so effortlessly. I do however believe it to be an essential key in living a more joyful life. Most things that we talk about, consume our time with, and allow to upset us do not truly matter. In the grand scheme of things you will not regret not purchasing that designer purse or pair of shoes. You will not care about the party you were not invited to. Your life is not any different than anyone else's. We are all born and we all die. We all need oxygen, food, water, shelter, and sleep. When someone does not know where his or her next meal is going to come from and you give it to him or her or when he or she has no place to stay and you provide a bed, you have no idea the gratitude you will receive and the joy you will feel in return. I have transformed my life slowly over the last year to make major strides in following these steps my grandmother displayed for me. I have not figured it all out, nor have I mastered these tools to the degree she so effortlessly displayed however, I believe awareness is key and I am on my way. I will say I am a much happier human than I was a year ago, living a life of greater joy and happiness. Follow these steps and join me on my journey to living the happiest life possible. Laugh more than you ever thought possible. Create memories and stories you will continue to tell for generations. Choose to live a life filled with optimal joy! Although, let me remind you, in order to do so you must first remember to keep your legs crossed and your zipper up.

THANK YOU

Ready to live the most joyful version of your life now?

Visit **www.StephGoldLifeCoach.com** to schedule a complimentary phone consultation

ACKNOWLEDGEMENTS

Thank you to everyone who has supported me on this journey. Thank you to my grandmother, who allowed me to record many of the long conversations we shared. Thank you for answering your phone at all hours of the day and night to chat. Thank you for calling me back when I would call you after a few drinks, in college, and taking the time to say hello or "Keep your legs crossed" to each one of my friends. Thank you to my cousins, uncles, aunts, and friends who allowed me to share these incredible stories you experienced with her.

Thank you to my editor, publishing team, supportive team of authors, and Angela to whom I could not have done this without. Thank you to Terri Mullins a dear family friend who coached me through final editing in making my manuscript print ready! Thank you to the Arizona sun that nurtured me in the first chapters of this book. Thank you the Saint Louis spring rain that motivated me to stay indoors and write the last few chapters of my book.

Thank you Ellen Degeneres for displaying to the world acceptance and unconditional love. Thank you for making daily dance a necessity and for honoring schools and teachers who make dreams like mine a reality. Your show continues to serve as my "afternoon break" and I am forever grateful for the inspiration and encouragement you supply to the world.

To the baristas at Starbucks, thank you for the countless "Oprah non fat Chi Tea Lattes" you made for me, during the writing process; they were incredibly appreciated. To my girlfriends and close female confidants-ladies, I waited my entire life to feel true friendship and I feel overwhelmingly blessed to have each and every one of you in my life. You women have been so pivotal during this time. You girls have lifted me, cried with me, laughed with me and I love you all endlessly. Thank you for your patience and words of encouragement.

Thank you to my mother for always believing in me. Your strength and encouragement this year especially, have left my heart so full of love and appreciation for you. You are my inspiration, drive, and beacon of unconditional love. Thank you endlessly.

To my father, who recently joined Gram in eternal peace, you will never know how your display of positivity has shaped me to my absolute core. There is not a day that goes by that I do not long to laugh with you again. My favorite place in the world remains on top of your shoulders. The love you gave me was enough to live off of for all of eternity.

Thank you to my friend, roommate and partner in crime. You hold many titles in my life but the one I cherish the most is brother. I prayed for you every night, I asked Santa for you every year, when you were not hidden in an Easter egg, you have never seen an angrier child. The world has never known someone more wanted and loved than you were even before you arrived. I am grateful for you beyond words and cherish our bond.

Thanks to the one that sat by me as I typed every word, listened with me as I replayed hours and hours of interview recordings, and never rushed me. Gizmo, you are the best companion and sweetest pup in the world. You bring me comfort and love, thank you for sticking by my side always.

I appreciate all the love, support, and encouragement I have received from family and friends. Thank you everyone who has encouraged and supported me over the years, the teachers who spent time editing every line of my papers and the strangers in passing that listened to my goal and encouraged me. I appreciate the outpouring of love and support tremendously from all those I have encountered.

ABOUT THE AUTHOR

One beautiful, sunny day in Fort Worth Texas, I walked into the psychology building, down the stairs and entered a room in the basement where class was held. This room was where one of my Psychology of Leadership courses took place. I can recall the room perfectly and the look on my favorite professor's face when I walked in the room. This class looked like any other, but it would not turn out that way.

Once everyone in the class had arrived my professor told us she was going to start class with an exercise. She turned off the lights in the classroom and asked that we close our eyes. I remember the darkness and stillness in the room. She proceeded to take us through a meditation. You walk into a church; there is a funeral of someone very close to you. Everyone you know is there. You walk down the aisle to pay your respects to the deceased and when you arrive at the front and peer inside the coffin you realize your body is inside. You take a seat and listen as people stand up and talk about you. What are they saying?

Our professor turned on the lights and asked us to write down what people said at our funeral. After a few minutes she asked us to stop. She had each of us review what we wrote and asked us to raise our hands if 70% or more of the things written were tasks, goals, and accomplishments we had yet to achieve. Every single person raised his or her hand. With that she said, "We never know how long our time is on earth, class is dismissed, go accomplish one item on your list." This exercise helped shape what I found to be truly important. It forced me to consider how I wanted to be remembered and not knowing how long I had, forced me to narrow my focus to living each day with purpose.

In another class this professor asked that we write down our life's mission statement. I determined mine to be "Positively impact the lives of as many people as possible." Having determined what was important to me and how I wanted to be remembered I quickly realized, having no idea how much time on earth I had, that I had a lot to do. At Texas Christian University where I attended college I took a position on the Panhellenic Executive Board in which one of my requirements was to hire a speaker to present to the Greek community.

I was very passionate about public speaking, a passion I had developed from attending Whitfield School where, as

President of the student body, I had spoken to the school often. Being given the opportunity to attend a speaker conference, as a college student, began to light a fire within me. After picking the brains of many motivational speakers at this conference they all gave the same response to my question, "Where do I start?" and their answer was, "Write a book."

This concept was insane to me in my early twenties. I had struggled with reading my entire life. I was given the title dyslexic at an early age, so you can imagine what an undertaking the thought of writing a book was for me. Overwhelming to say the least. When I thought of writing a book my grandmother came to mind because of her ability to tell a story and the way people gravitated toward her. I had every intention of writing a book on her life but the words never came. I won't refer to it as "Writer's block" more lacking in my own life experience.

I understood how amazing my Gram was and how fun her stories were to hear but it was not until she passed that I realized how desperately the world needed her perspective on life. It was not what happened to her it was how she interpreted what happened that made her story so magnificent. My passion for living my best life now and being as happy and joyful as possible has turned into my top priority. I am on a mission to help as many others as possible do the same! Join me on my mission to choose joy!